Mommy Can Do It

Mommy Can Do It

✦

A Do-It-Herself Guide to Baby-Proofing

Kelly A. Smith

iUniverse, Inc.
New York Lincoln Shanghai

Mommy Can Do It
A Do-It-Herself Guide to Baby-Proofing

iUniverse books may be ordered through booksellers or by contacting:

iUniverse
2021 Pine Lake Road, Suite 100
Lincoln, NE 68512
www.iuniverse.com
1-800-Authors (1-800-288-4677)

The information provided in this book is not intended as a substitute for competent adult supervision and will not prevent all accidents, injuries, or deaths. The authors, publishers and contributors disclaim any liability arising directly or indirectly from the use of this book.

ISBN-13: 978-0-595-41076-7 (pbk)
ISBN-13: 978-0-595-85436-3 (ebk)
ISBN-10: 0-595-41076-6 (pbk)
ISBN-10: 0-595-85436-2 (ebk)

Printed in the United States of America

For my husband for helping me make my dreams come true everyday. For my son for being my inspiration. For my parents for their never-ending support and encouragement

Contents

Introduction

As Mommies, we can do almost everything that our children need. We nurture them, feed them, bathe them, play with them and love them. We can do almost anything—until it comes to baby proofing. As soon as we see the words "drill a 1/16" pilot hole" most Mommies run screaming for Daddy. The idea of using a drill or screwdriver sometimes seems as foreign and daunting as overhauling an engine or building a house from the ground up. If you feel that way, you're not alone. I've worked with thousands of families over the years as retail customers and in my home childproofing business and most of the time Dad is the main contact person when it comes to baby proofing. In fact, before I became a professional baby proofer, my husband installed our first baby safety gate and I stayed as far away as possible.

Believe it or not, childproofing your home is something that you can do. This book has been written as a guide for women; A guide to help women overcome their fears of tools and empower themselves to learn to keep their children safe at home. This book will help you learn what child safety products are appropriate for your home, your child, and your budget and will help walk you step-by-step through the process of childproofing your home.

This book has been organized so that each chapter focuses on one room of the home or other problem area. If you have a certain area that you are concerned about, simply turn to that chapter and read on! There is also a comprehensive childproofing checklist in Chapter 12 to help you on your way to developing what I call a "Totsafe" home. Each chapter includes tips and tricks for childproofing and woman-friendly advice for installation and inspiration.

I hope you'll enjoy this book and the freedom and empowerment that will come from looking back on what you have done and being able to say, "I did that." You can do it—most childproofing items don't even require the use of a drill, and those that do require drilling can be simple if you know the right steps to take. This book is about empowering yourself, doing something that you normally wouldn't take charge of and showing yourself that you have the strength and courage to follow through on one of the most important tasks for parents—keeping your little one safe. By creating what I call a "Totsafe" home, you'll be able to focus on the things that really matter like playing, loving, and learning.

1

How and Why to Childproof

If you're a parent, you've probably already done it—you buy what you think looks like a great child safety product only to get it home and have it not fit where you wanted it to, or to have your child pull it right off. Several trips to the local baby store and hundreds of dollars later you finally find the right product to help keep your precious little one (who doubles as the devil when no one other than you is looking!) safe.

If you haven't encountered this situation yet, consider yourself lucky—and warned. As parents, we all know how important it is to keep our children safe. Safe, happy, and healthy, right? So, we know we want our kids to be safe—but what we don't always know is *how* to keep them safe. Too many times people have an appropriate child safety item still in the package, but haven't gotten around to installing it yet because hubby is out of town or works late hours and hasn't been able to find time. Newsflash—you can do this, ladies! In about the time it takes for your baby to take a nap or two, you can make your home safe for your child for years to come without breaking the bank—or your nails.

Some parents think that if they install childproofing products they may as well turn their house into one big padded room. Do you need to turn your home into a padded room? The answer is no. Kids actually need to be introduced to different colors, textures, sounds, etc. to learn how things work. At certain ages, they need to be able to "pull" themselves up on furniture and navigate a stairway under adult supervision to help develop gross motor skills. The keys to keeping children at this stage safe are supervision and appropriate childproofing for the age and needs of your child. Children need constant, appropriate adult supervision at all times—no matter how much childproofing you do in your home, supervision is still the number one means to prevent injury that I know of. So why use childproofing products at all?

Toddler-hood is a very inquisitive time for children, and as such can be hazardous. Thousands of children are injured in the home each year, and an enormous percentage of these injuries could have been prevented with proper adult supervision and childproofing of the home. Throughout this book, I will discuss child safety products that have been designed to increase the amount of time it takes for a child to get into an unsafe situation, giving caregivers added moments to move children out of harm's way.

Let me say that again—child safety products are designed to increase the amount of time it takes for a child to get into an unsafe situation, giving caregivers added moments to move children out of harm's way. Using childproofing products is not a guarantee that your child will never get hurt, or find him/herself in an unsafe situation. Childproofing products help prevent accidents and injuries by giving caregivers an increased amount of time to move the child away from a possible danger.

Homes are not created with the safety of children in mind. There are hundreds of hazards in the home that create problems for children—from electrical outlets to stairways, from sharp fireplace hearths to open banisters, homes have a wide array of areas that can be hazards to children. If you go to your local baby specialty retail store or search for "childproofing products" on the internet you'll find thousands of products designed to help create a safer area for children.

So how is a parent supposed to know which safety items to use? Is there a difference between a $150 child safety gate and another $25 one? How do I keep my kid safe when I'm at a hotel or at the grandparent's house? These are all questions that this book has been written to answer.

Throughout this book you will find answers to some of the commonly asked child safety questions that I have received over the years (and there are many). My answers focus on helping you learn what is needed to make a safe home environment for your child. Child safety does not need to be costly, but it does need your attention. Many of my suggestions have no costs associated with them at all. Others do. I will try to show specific products to help explain what to do for certain situations—which I have personally used in my own home and in my childproofing business throughout the years. I hope that this book will help save you some time, money, and energy that could be better spent with your children and help you create a safe environment for your child at home and away.

Please remember, this book is for reference only, and following the recommendations in this book will not prevent all accidents, injuries, or deaths to children.

Helping Dad (and grandparents and friends and everyone else) understand why childproofing is necessary.

According to the Safe Kids Worldwide, there are 11.8 million medical visits for unintentional injury (accidents) every year for children ages 14 and under. Unintentional injury is the number one killer of children ages 14 and under—claiming approximately 5,600 lives each year. That's over 15 children per day.

What is unintentional injury? Unintentional injuries, in general, are accidents. Drowning, falls, motor vehicle injuries, burns, poisoning, dog bites, airway obstructions, and others are included in this list. In 2001, drowning was the number one leading killer of children ages 1 to 4.

This book will focus on using child safety products and supervision as a means of helping to prevent these unintentional injuries from occurring. Childproofing is something that every parent can do. It doesn't need to be costly—some homes require very few childproofing products. Many of the suggestions that I offer require no cost. Sometimes childproofing is as simple as moving a piece of furniture over 2 inches to cover an electrical outlet or removing a sharp piece of furniture from the room to prevent head injuries.

Unfortunately, most homes are not made with child safety in mind. Most homes have open, easily accessible stairways, unsecured electrical outlets, open access to bathrooms and other water sources, and unlocked cabinets with poisonous substances. These areas all need attention to keep kids out of harm's way.

"Is Childproofing Really Necessary?" "We didn't have that when I was growing up, and we turned out just fine."

I've encountered them myself—people who will question why you would want to childproof your home because they remember when they were kids (or had young kids) and didn't bother to childproof. Some of these people believe that childproofing is not necessary or that "kids will learn."

According to Safe Kids Worldwide, injuries to children happen most when a task's demands exceed the child's ability to safely complete it. For instance, if a 9 month old that is learning to walk attempts to navigate a large staircase, there is an increased chance of injury due to a lack of developmental ability. This child cannot "learn" to correctly navigate the stairway. He or she does not have the muscle or mental capability to complete this task safely. He or she must developmentally grow and with this growth and maturity of ability will eventually be able to ascend and descend a staircase with much less of a chance of injury.

Unintentional injury, although it is the leading cause of death to children under the age of 14, has decreased over the years. From 1987 to 2000, the death rate from accidents dropped almost 40 percent. There has been a significant drop in accident rates, but there is still more to be done. For that person out there who is walking around saying "We didn't have that when I was growing up, and we turned out just fine." I say—do you know how many people didn't turn out just fine, or didn't make it at all?

As parents, it is our job to help keep this downward trend in injury continuing. The 11.8 million medical visits per year are still too many injuries (and those are only the ones that get reported). There are probably thousands or millions more incidents every year that don't require medical attention, or simply don't get the attention they need. Approximately 15 children are dying everyday due to accidents that could have been prevented.

We all have the ability to create safe environments for our children. Children will still fall and get scraped knees, but it is my hope that we can help prevent the serious injuries that require hospital visits, and of course, help prevent deaths caused by accidents.

This book focuses on children ages 1 to 4. For this age group, Safe Kids reports that the leading cause of accidental death is drowning, which accounts for 27% of the deaths in this age category. Children under the age of 4 have the highest likelihood of injury and death due to motor vehicle accidents, pedestrian injury, choking and suffocation (airway obstruction), fire and burns, falls, and poisoning than all other children under the age of 14.

Children ages 1 to 4 are almost constantly on the move, wanting to try new things and new abilities. When a newly walking 1 year old encounters a bucket of water, he or she doesn't have the thought process to assess drowning danger. He or she will go for the bucket of water out of curiosity regardless of any danger the water presents. Two year olds who are left to navigate stairways unattended may fall when trying to carry too many toys and becoming off balance.

These are just a few of the reasons to childproof your home. I recommend childproofing be done when children are 3 to 6 months of age—before baby begins to crawl. Don't wait for your child to start opening cabinets or trying to climb the stairs before you childproof your home. Do it as soon as you can, and as thoroughly as possible to help prevent the number one cause of injury to children (unintentional injuries).

The checklist included later in the book has been designed by me through my years of working one-on-one with parents to help them keep their children safe with my childproofing company. The checklist has been designed to be as thorough as possible, but please remember, that the checklist is only a reference, and will not cover every child safety risk in the home, nor will it prevent all accidents and injuries.

2

Tools—The Woman's Guide to Tools

So now that you're reading this book, you should start to feel confident that you can go out and buy some child safety products with the knowledge that you're about to gain, and you should be ready to start installing those products...right? Do your hands start to shake and does your forehead break into a cold sweat at the thought of drilling a hole into the wall or cabinet? This chapter will help you become familiar with some of the most frequently used tools in the baby proofing professional's toolbox. Don't worry...working with tools can be fun. You may find that once you get started working with tools, you might actually enjoy it.

Tools you'll most likely need when installing safety products:

- **Drill**—both battery-operated (cordless) or electric (corded) are fine. If you're installing cabinet latches you'll most likely want an electric (corded) drill, or you'll have to take breaks to charge your drill battery.

- **Drill Bits**—you'll need several sizes of bits. You'll most likely need drill bits that are made for drilling into wood. There are also bits called masonry bits that are made for if you need to drill into brick, concrete, etc. If you don't have drill bits on hand, they can be purchased at your local hardware store—but be careful—they must fit into the "chuck" of your drill. If you're unsure, take your drill with you and ask for help.

- **Screwdriver**—you can generally use either a manual or electric/battery operated screwdriver for most baby-proofing jobs. Again, if you're installing several cabinet latches or drawer latches, you'll most likely want to use an electric or battery operated screwdriver so you don't wake up the next morning feeling like your arms are going to fall off from all the turning!

- **Screwdriver Bits**—You're most likely going to need screwdriver bits that will fit crosshead (AKA "Phillips") screws. You may also need a screwdriver bit that will fit a slot-head screw, called a flat bladed screwdriver bit. Most screwdrivers include bits that will fit perfectly with the screwdriver, but if you need to purchase something, again, take your screwdriver with you to the hardware store and ask an expert for help.

- **Wrenches**—When installing baby safety gates, you may need a wrench to tighten nuts and bolts. Most gates that require use of wrenches include the correct size wrench. In the event that you need a different type of wrench, adjustable wrenches are available to fit many different sizes of nuts and bolts and are easily used.

- **Stud Finder**—A "stud" is the structural wood behind the wall in your home that holds the drywall, panel, etc. to the wall. Most baby safety gates need to be installed into studs in the wall, and furniture safety straps also need to be installed into studs to ensure a proper, secure installation. A stud finder is a device that when slid along the wall will either beep or light up to tell you where the wooden studs are behind the wall. Most stud finders include directions on the back of them to show you how to properly locate a stud. In some homes, you may be able to locate the location of studs in the wall by finding "nail pops" or areas where drywall screws are sticking out and create a bump in the drywall. Always test with a screw to make sure that there is indeed a stud where you think there is one—if you start to install a screw into the wall and either can't get it tight or if it continues to spin once it's fully into the wall, chances are that you've missed the stud and need to try again.

- **Saw**—In the unlikely event that you need to trim a gate installation kit (a piece of wood) to fit an area, you may need to use either a handsaw or power saw to trim the wood. I highly recommend that someone who is skilled with a saw do this type of work or that you ask for help from someone with experience before using a saw for the first time. Make sure to wear your safety goggles at all times and use extreme caution with the saw—and never allow your child around a saw!

- **Level**—a leveling device may be needed to ensure that a safety gate is being installed correctly. If not level, many safety gates will not close and latch correctly. Most levels are very simple to use and read. Simply set the level on or next to the item that you are trying to level and look inside to make sure the air bubble in the water is in the middle of two lines. Adjust the item side-to-side or up and down to adjust for level.

- **Measuring Tape**—the use of a measuring tape is going to be absolutely necessary for several different baby-proofing items in the home, including measuring areas for baby safety gates, and finding out the measurements of tables and fireplace hearths for edge cushions. If you're trying to use a measuring tape when no one else is around, simply 'hook' the end of the tape onto the edge of the area that you're measuring and pull the tape from the other end to get the measurement of the area. If the tape measure won't stay hooked at the end, simply place something heavy on the end while pulling, or use your foot to hold it down if it's a small area.

- **Eye Goggles**—eye protection is extremely important when working with power tools. Wood pieces may splinter off, and going flying—and of course your eyes are the targets. Wear eye protection at all times when installing baby-proofing products to help protect your eyes.

- **Boots or shoes**—be sure to wear comfortable, non-slip shoes that can help protect your feet and toes from injuries. You may be surprised at how often you drop a screw onto your foot or drop the drill and have it almost slam right into your foot. Wear protective shoes or boots at all times when using tools.

- **Babysitter**—having a responsible person around that you trust to watch your child while you're focusing on making your home "Totsafe" can be an invaluable tool to help you complete your job in as little time as possible, and, if you pick the right person, may also be able to offer suggestions if you become stuck or frustrated. It's important that you let your babysitter know to keep your child away from the area(s) where you're working and that there may be tools laying around that your child should not have access to. If you have a nanny or frequent babysitter, having that person in the home while you're installing the products may be useful in more ways than one—you have a babysitter to keep your child safe while you're busy and you can teach your babysitter to use the products properly right away once you've installed them.

Most of the products that you will install will come with all the necessary hardware (screws, washers, nuts, bolts, etc.) that you need. You may find, however, that during installation screws may break or you may lose washers down the heat vents. If you need replacement hardware, I recommend that you contact the company that manufacturers the item and request a replacement hardware pack or ask for suggestions regarding replacement hardware that you can pick up at your local hardware store.

Before attempting to use tools for the first time, I suggest putting on your eye protective goggles and shoes and practicing on scrap pieces of wood and/or drywall. Practice screwing screws into wood that's behind drywall to get a feel for screwing into studs to help you identify what it should feel like. You may also want to practice using the drill using several different sizes of drill bits. An important thing to know before drilling into walls and other painted surfaces—older homes (those built before 1978) may have lead in the paint that may become loosened during drilling. This lead is toxic. If your home was built before 1978, have your local health department come to your home or request a lead testing kit from them or purchase one at your local hardware store or online.

You'll also want to practice using the stud finder to locate wooden studs in the wall. A great place to test a stud finder is in the garage. Read the instructions regarding how to properly locate a stud and then give it a try, following the directions. Mark the place where the stud should be located, then use your drill with a small drill bit installed to see if there is, indeed, a wooden stud in that location. If the drill doesn't feel like it hit a "soft spot" or if you place a screw in that is larger than the hole you drill and it installs tightly, chances are good that you've correctly located a stud. Congratulations, I knew you could do it!

Prior to installing any baby-proofing product, familiarize yourself with the instructions and make sure you understand them fully before proceeding. If you have questions, call the manufacturer for help—many of the manufacturers of these products have excellent customer service and some have trained customer service professionals who have personally installed the products in test facilities. For questions relating to your home specifically, ask a baby-proofing professional for suggestions (many will offer suggestions for free) or ask at your local hardware store. My philosophy is "ask twice, drill once!"

An important piece of advice: if at any time you become overwhelmed or frustrated during the installation of baby-proofing products, take a break and/or ask for help. Move on to another project or go do something that you enjoy for a while and come back to the other thing at a later time when you've had a chance to cool off. In that time, you may also be able to figure out what you're having a hard time with and may even find an easy solution once you've relaxed.

3

Baby Safety Gates—Stairways, doorways, and beyond

Baby safety gates are normally the first things parents think of when baby-proofing their homes. Baby safety gates come in many different shapes and sizes and are made of several different materials. You'll find that the majority of baby safety gates are made of metal, wood, or plastic. I highly recommend looking for baby safety gates that are made out of metal or very sturdy wood that will not break or crack. Every baby safety gate has dimensions and features that may or may not work with the area that you need them to. Also, be sure to look for the Juvenile Products Manufacturers Association (JPMA) seal of approval on all baby safety gates to ensure they meet the appropriate safety standards.

Take a look at your home and jot down the areas where you need baby safety gates. Look at the tops and bottoms of stairways—children should not have access to stairways unattended until they are successfully capable of navigating stairs safely. You may also want to use a baby safety gate to divide rooms, block off hallways, kitchens, and exercise equipment and may also use gates to keep children in safe areas such as bedrooms or play areas.

Choosing and installing baby safety gates can be one of the most daunting tasks facing parents when baby-proofing their home—especially women. Most hardware installed baby safety gates require the use of a drill and screwdriver and also may require additional hardware or installation kits in spaces with special circumstances like thick baseboards, banister rails and wrought iron railings. There are three main steps to help you choose and install the right baby safety gate for your space. There is no perfect gate for all situations, but using these three steps should help you find an appropriate gate for your space:

1) **Consider—where is the gate going**? If it is going at the top of a stairway, you will want to look for a hardware mounted (screwed into the wall) gate, <u>never use</u>

a pressure-mounted gate at the top of the stairs. If the gate will be used to block off a room, or prevent a child from climbing up the stairs, you may be able to choose from hardware mounted and pressure mounted gates.

2) **Determine—what size is the opening where the gate will go**? You will need to measure the opening where your gate will go, both width of the opening, and height of the opening. Child safety gates all have specific dimensions that they will fit. You need to find a gate that will securely fit in your space. Some gates require extension kits to fit larger areas.

3) **Decide—are there any special circumstances in the space that you need the baby gate to go**? If you have a banister, molding, hollow wall (drywall or plaster with no stud behind it), or wrought iron railing, you may need the use of a gate installation kit to create a proper mounting surface. Kits are also available to mount a baby gate to banister posts without creating drill and screw holes. Please see more information about gate installation kits below.

Using these three factors can help you make an informed decision on choosing proper baby gates for your space. Please remember that most gates are appropriate for ages between six months and three years of age. This may be more or less for certain gates and manufacturers. As a rule of thumb, if the top of the baby gate is at or below a child's shoulder height, it is time to discontinue use of the gate.

A great tip for securing stairways to basements: If there is a door at the top of the stairway, use a childproof door lock on the door that is out of the child's reach. This will prevent access to the stairway longer than a baby safety gate, and will also help prevent you from having to install another safety gate.

Mounting a baby gate to spaces with hollow walls, wrought iron railings, banisters & moldings/baseboards:

Gate Installation Kits are kits created to help build a mountable surface for a baby safety gate in spaces that have moldings, banisters/newel posts, hollow walls, and wrought iron railings. They are needed in almost all gate installations where the gate is not being mounted in a wood framed door opening. They are installed prior to the baby safety gate. Most gate installation kits are appropriate for hardware mounted and pressure mounted safety gates. At the time of this writing, there are also kits to help you mount a safety gate to stairway newel posts without creating holes.

There are four main types of baby safety gates: hardware mounted, pressure mounted, gates for extra wide and irregular spaces, and travel safety gates.

Hardware Mounted Baby Safety Gates:

The Stairway Special by Cardinal Gates

Hardware mounted gates are secured into a structural part of your home with screws and are considered to be the most secure baby gates, and are often the most daunting task for parents who are trying to childproof their homes. Hardware mounted gates must be installed into a solid location such as between a wood framed doorway or between a banister and wall with a stud behind it. They are the most secure option for stairways, to block off doorways or hallways, almost any situation. Hardware mounted (screwed in) gates are the only recommended option for the top of the stairs. If there is not a solid surface where you want to mount a baby gate, please learn more about Gate Installation Kits. The holes that are created from hardware-mounted gates tend to be small and in most cases are easily filled when use of the gate is discontinued.

Installation of hardware-mounted gates can be easier than most women think. First, use the steps above to help you choose the right gate for your space. Make sure the dimensions of the gate fit the space that you need. Extensions for the gate may be necessary to fit your space. Most hardware-mounted gates require only a few tools, such as a drill to create holes in the wall or banister, screwdriver to install the gate into the wall, and sometimes require a wrench to tighten bolts.

Look for the Juvenile Products Manufacturers Association (JPMA) seal of approval on baby safety gates to ensure they meet the necessary safety guidelines. *"I need a child safety gate for the top of a staircase but one side is wall and the other is a metal handrail (wrought iron). I cannot use a pressure system because of the stair use and I cannot use a hardware mount system because of the metal railing side. What can I do?"*

A wrought iron railing is common in stairways of many homes and apartments. For mounting a gate to this type of railing, try two of the Kidco Safety Gate Installation Kit K10, which can be used to create a 'frame' around the wrought iron railing. Hardware mounted gates can then be mounted onto this 'frame.'

Pressure Mounted Baby Safety Gates:

Sure and Secure™ Extra-Tall Walk-Thru Gate by Summer Infant

This type of gate is often the most sought after gate because no holes are created when using this type of gate, and little or no tools are needed during installation of these gates. These gates have cushioned pads that press against the mounting surface to create a tight fit. They are great for blocking off rooms & hallways, blocking access at the bottom of the stairs (they are not for use at the top of the stairs) these baby gates need to be mounted between two solid surfaces straight across from each other.

Many people ask me why pressure mounted baby gates should not be used at the top of the stairs, where many people wish not to create holes. The answer is this: Because pressure-mounted baby gates create a very strong force on the surfaces that they are mounted between, the pressure can 'push out' on the two surfaces enough to eventually slip out of place with force. Pressure mounted gates must be checked frequently to ensure that they are remaining tight in the space, and manufacturers (as well as myself) do not suggest using this type of gate at the top of the stairs. Hardware-mounted gates are a much more secure option for this location, and can generally hold up to children banging and climbing on them. Luckily, the holes that are created from hardware-mounted gates tend to be small and are easily filled when use of the gate is discontinued.

Baby Safety Gates for Extra-Wide and Irregular Spaces:

ConfigureGate® by Kidco, Inc.

These are baby safety gates created to fit extra-wide spaces, and spaces that have special circumstances. If you have a stairway in your home that has a rounded stair at the bottom, this type of gate may be what you may need. Other areas that this type of gate is great for are to surround exercise equipment, fireplaces, Christmas trees, and as room dividers. The gate shown above has several panels that can be set at angles from each other, adding extra strength compared to a straight safety gate.

Travel Safety Gates:

Gateway® To Go by Kidco, Inc.

Keep your little one safe away from home, too. These safety gates are made collapsible for easy travel to hotels, bed and breakfasts, and grandparents house. These gates are pressure-mounted gates so no holes are created. The Gateway To Go by Kidco can be collapsed to fit into a small suitcase, which can be very helpful for traveling parents.

In my professional childproofing business, there are certain steps that I take to ensure a proper installation of child safety gates. After I have followed the three steps to choosing a baby safety gate and am ready to install the gate in the space I:

- **Install gate installation kits on one or both sides (if needed) of the stairway.** Using gate installation kits is required in most baby safety gate installations that are not being mounted directly between two wooden doorframes. Installation kits may be needed on both sides of the gate, or on just one side depending on the special circumstances of your area, and the type of gate that you have purchases. If you have a hardware-mounted gate and can't find a stud in the wall anywhere, you'll need to install a gate installation kit into the wall using the included hollow wall anchors. Make sure that the screws or straps used to install the installation kit won't be in the way of the hardware for the baby gate.

- **Install the gate onto the gate installation kit or directly into a stud. If pressure mounting, mount the gate between two strong, solid surfaces.** Be sure to follow the manufacturers instructions carefully to ensure proper installation. If you have any questions—call the manufacturer immediately. Don't try to do something that may bend or break the gate or hardware or that may not hold up in the future and cause injury.

- **Test the gate, test the gate, test the gate**—Open and close the gate repeatedly (I'm talking like 20 times and then again every time you go up and down the stairs) to make sure that it latches and opens correctly every time. Make adjustments according to the gate manufacturers instructions to help get the gate working properly.

- **Instruct anyone who watches your child**—teach all caregivers how to properly open and close the gate—never let anyone climb over the gate—it's a bad example for your child and the person may trip over the gate and fall. Make sure caregivers know that your child should not be allowed near the gate without proper adult supervision.

- **Never allow your child to climb or pull the gate**—even though baby safety gates are meant to help prevent falls down the stairs, etc. most can not hold up to a child climbing and pulling on them. Most gates have plastic pieces that can bend or break, and if the gate was not properly installed into studs in the walls, etc. the gate may pull out and fall on your child, or make your child fall down the stairs. Remove gates from the home immediately if your child climbs them and when the gates are at or below your child's shoulder level.

4

Electrical Safety—Keeping Jr. from getting the "shock" of his life

With all the electrical outlet safety devices out there, finding appropriate safety items for electrical outlets can be a large concern for parents. Children can receive painful shocks and burns and can even be killed by the shocks from electrical outlets and appliances.

When my son was around three, we went to help a friend unpack some boxes and clean when they were moving into their new home. The only things in the house were taped up boxes, a garbage can and a set of keys. I was working on cleaning the bathroom and my friend was in the kitchen cleaning while my son played in the eat-in kitchen area. While my friend's back was turned, my son found the keys and decided that the unprotected electrical outlet looked like a keyhole. Yes, he did stick the key into the outlet and did receive quite a shock. Luckily, he was not severely injured, but it did serve as a reminder of how fast kids can get into trouble.

The following is a guide to the electrical safety products available, to help you decide which are most appropriate for your home. First of all, there are two main types of outlet styles that may show up in your home—Standard outlets and Decorator outlets. Most homes have standard outlets. You can easily determine this by simply looking at your outlets. Decorator Outlets have 2 screws, one at top, and one at bottom. Standard outlets have one screw, in the middle of the outlet. You need to know which type of outlet your home has for many of the outlet safety products that we are going to discuss:

Outlet Covers:

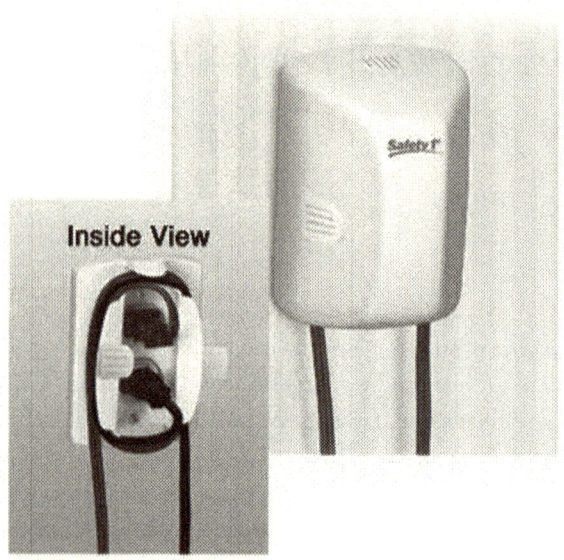

Inside View

Outlet Cover with Cord Shortener by Safety 1st

I suggest outlet covers for outlets that have items plugged in all the time (i.e. a lamp), that you don't need frequent access to, or for areas where you have large adaptors (like at the computer) plugged in. Outlet covers are not easily figured out by toddlers, either, which adds to their value significantly. Outlet covers can be purchased for standard and decorator outlets. As a general rule, if the product doesn't specify which type of outlet, it is usually for standard outlets. If they are for decorator outlets, they normally list that in the description. Products made for standard outlets generally can not be used with decorator outlets and vice versa, so make certain you are clear which type they are for before you purchase.

There are several types of outlet covers available that will cover a regular electrical cord, but will also cover large adapters and other irregular electrical items that may be found in the home.

Outlet Plates:

Safe-Plate™ by Mommy's Helper, Inc.

Outlet plates have been a long-time favorite in our home childproofing business for outlets that are frequently used (i.e. the outlet you use to plug in vacuum, then remove it). Outlet plates replace your existing outlet plate and have a 'door' that slides closed to cover the outlet as soon as an item is unplugged. These are also very difficult for little ones to figure out.

Outlet Plates are easy to install. However, I do recommend shutting off the electricity to each outlet before attempting to install any electrical safety device. Once you've shut off the electricity using the circuit breakers (which are normally found in the basement or utility area) test the outlet using a lamp or other electronic device to ensure the electricity is actually off. After you've confirmed the electricity to the outlet is indeed off, go ahead and remove the outlet plate that's currently on the outlet using a screwdriver. Set that plate aside, and replace it with the child safety outlet plate. If the safety plate included insulating foam, install that onto the inside of the outlet around the outside of the plug receptacles prior to installing the safety plate.

Outlet Plugs:

Electrical Outlet Caps by Kidco, Inc.

Outlet plugs are suggested for outlets that are normally left unused. Outlet plugs fit snugly inside outlets to prevent access. Outlet plugs can be used interchangeably with standard and decorator outlets. Children seem to figure out these types of devices sooner than outlet plates and covers.

Office areas, entertainment centers, and many other places around the home pose risks to children with electrical equipment. Small children may try to chew on electrical cords or try to pull them out of the wall or equipment. Power strips and surge protectors pose a safety risk to children. With up to ten electrical appliances plugged in at one time, surge protectors and power strips can seem like an interesting toy to children who do not understand their risks.

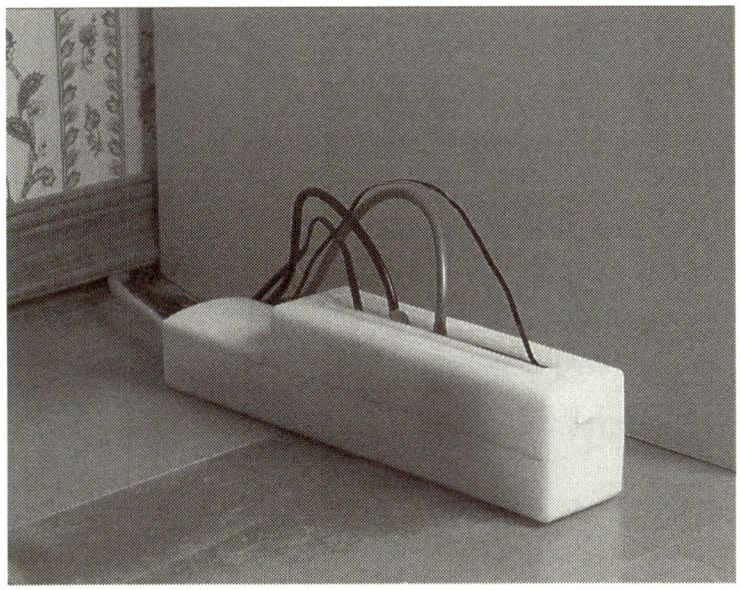

Power Strip Safety Cover by Mommy's Helper

Install power strip covers like the Power Strip Cover by Safety 1st on all power strips and surge protectors to help prevent children from pulling on and removing plugs from the outlets. Some power strip covers can be attached to the floor or to the wall behind a desk to help keep them out of children's reach.

In addition to the electrical risks associated with cords and appliances, cords also pose a strangulation risk to children. Telephone cords, lamps and other electronic equipment have cords that may dangle or hang or even lay on the floor where children can access them. These items should be removed from reach of children to minimize the risk of injury.

Securing outlets is one of the easiest things to do in the home. Many times, parents can strategically place furniture in front of outlets so that the outlets are no longer accessible. Simply unplugging electrical items, plugging the outlet receptacle with outlet plugs, and removing electrical items from children's reach can decrease the risk of injuries by amazing amounts. Organize electrical cords behind entertainment centers and computer areas and move them out of reach.

- Determine if your home has standard (one screw) or decorator (two screws) outlets.

- Install outlet covers, plates, or plugs as necessary to prevent access to outlets.

- Secure electrical cords out of the reach of children.

- Block outlets with sturdy, heavy furniture.

- Place power strip covers on all power strips and surge protectors and secure out of reach

- Install cord covers over all electrical cords in reach to prevent children from biting on cords.

- Wrap and organize cords behind entertainment centers.

- Shorten electric cords from lamps and other appliances using cord shorteners to keep them out of reach.

5

The Family Room

It's the room in the home where you spend most of your time and, most likely, so does your child. The family room is a place where family members play, rest, and do a variety of other tasks. Not surprisingly, there are many things in most family rooms and living areas that are not safe for children. Some problems are with the room itself, like exposed electrical outlets and sharp fireplace hearths. Other child safety issues may come from what you bring into the room, like older children's toys, candles, breakables, and even plants. With a little bit of work, you can make the family room a safe haven for your little one.

Electrical outlet risks are probably one of the easiest concerns to manage in the family room. Often, a piece of furniture can be moved in front of an outlet to block access to it. Just make sure the furniture is heavy enough to ensure that your child won't move it, or that your child can't get behind it. If in doubt, install outlet plugs, covers or plates on the outlets.

If you have an entertainment center, chances are that you've got one heck of a jumble of cords behind it. If the cords are out of reach behind a heavy entertainment center or cabinet that can't be moved, they should be fine. One thing you do need to pay some attention to is attaching the entertainment center to the wall to help prevent it from tipping onto your child and using straps to attach your television and any other heavy appliance to your entertainment center (see the Furniture Safety chapter for more information). Children are very curious around televisions and are likely to attempt to climb the entertainment center and pull on the television. When my nephew was four years old, he pulled their 32" television right off of the entertainment center and it came crashing down all the way to the floor. Luckily, my nephew hung onto the entertainment center (which was strapped to a stud in the wall) like a monkey and the television didn't land on him or his two other siblings. Needless to say, my brother-in-law installed appliance safety straps right away after that!

All heavy furniture in the home including entertainment centers, armoires, bookcases, dressers, and microwave carts should be strapped to a stud in the wall using furniture safety brackets. Furniture safety brackets can be purchased at most child specialty stores and hardware stores and simply screw into the piece of furniture and into a stud in the wall. There is a strap that goes between the pieces that are attached to the furniture and wall to help prevent tipping.

If you have live plants in your family room, you may want to remove them when your child is young to keep her from ingesting parts of the plant and dirt/ fertilizer, and from knocking the plant over. Many common plants found in and around the home are poisonous if ingested—check with your child's doctor for a list of poisonous plants and be sure to remove any plants from the home that are on the list.

Do you like to open your windows to air out the house? Open windows, even first story windows, can be a fall hazard to children. Thousands of children are injured/killed each year due to window falls, and these falls can easily be prevented. Any window open more than about 4" can pose a fall hazard to children—install window locks or guards to keep children from having access to windows and never leave children unattended around open windows.

Sharp edged tables like coffee tables, sofa tables, end tables, and even entertainment center corners can cause injuries to children. Little ones who are learning to walk are likely to pull up on furniture and if the edges and corners are exposed, they may become injured. Installing edge and corner cushioning is a simple and effective way to help prevent this type of injury. Simply measure the circumference (distance around the edge) of the table and order the correct size or amount of edge and corner cushions. FYI: using corner cushions alone is an ineffective use of the product. Children can easily remove corner cushions alone by peeling them off. Use them in conjunction with edge cushions.

If you have older children, their toys may actually be a hazard to your younger children. Toys made for older children often have small parts that are not safe for young children. Remove all unsafe toys from the family room.

Knick-knacks, vases, glass candle holders, picture frames, and even CD cases can cause injuries to children and should be removed from the family room or moved out of the reach of children.

- Install electrical safety items on all electrical outlets or place stable, heavy furniture in front of outlets.

- Secure electric cords from entertainment centers, lamps, etc. out of reach of children.

- Attach all heavy and/or unstable pieces of furniture (including entertainment centers, bookcases, cabinets, etc.) to studs in the wall using anti-tip furniture safety straps

- Attach all electrical appliances, such as the TV, to a sturdy piece of furniture using anti-slip safety straps.

- Remove or cover houseplants—some are poisonous to children, and many have fertilizer in the soil.

- Secure all windows to prevent falls using window safety locks or guards.

- Remove tables, etc. with sharp edges and corners or install protective cushioning.

- Install a safety gate around fireplaces and/or install protective cushioning on sharp edges and corners. Install a fireplace door lock to keep children out of the fireplace.

6

Kitchen Safety

Kitchens can be one of the most hazardous rooms in your home for children. In most kitchens there are sharp objects like knives and scissors, poisonous cleaners, glass and heavy objects, plastic materials, heavy unstable furniture, and many other hazards. I highly recommend installing a baby safety gate to block access to the kitchen in addition to installing proper child safety items in the room. (Return to Chapter three for tips on installing baby safety gates).

Never hold your child when you are working in the kitchen. Children are very curious about their surroundings and may try to grab hot foods or sharp items that could pose a risk of injury. Many parents create a "child safe" cupboard so that their child can explore the items inside that cupboard safely while Mom or Dad are working in the kitchen. Although that sounds like a wonderful way for a child to explore and learn about his surroundings, children do not associate the idea that it is okay for them to play in one cabinet, but not another. He or she may try to get into cupboards that are not safe for them the moment Mom or Dad isn't looking. Keeping children out of the kitchen all together is the safest approach.

Stove Guard by Prince Lionheart

Stoves are a large source of injuries to children. Hot stovetops and ovens look very appealing to children who want to learn about what is happening. Most toddlers do not have the developmental capacity to learn that something that is hot will hurt them and should be kept away from the stove and oven at all times—even when they are not in use. Always use the back burners when cooking and make sure that panhandles are pointing toward the back of the stove. Special guards can be installed onto the stove to help prevent access to burners as well as pots and pans.

Clear View Stove Knob Covers by Safety 1st

Most children are very curious about stove knobs and will try to turn the knobs any chance they get, which can allow them to turn on the gas or electric stove without a parent's knowledge. Gas can create a fire hazard and turning on an electric stove can also create a fire hazard. Use stove knob safety devises to help prevent access to burner knobs. These items are easily installed by removing the existing stove knob, slipping the cover behind the knob and replacing the knob back onto the stove. The cover will then clamp over the knob to help prevent access.

Fridge Guard by Parent Units

The use of adhesive locks on the refrigerator/freezer is recommended to prevent little ones from getting into food & drinks they should not have and to help prevent tipping of refrigerators onto children. These items are installed to the refrigerator with a heavy-duty adhesive tape.

Sharp knives and other sharp objects should be stored in locked drawers that children cannot reach. Plastic bags and plastic wrap can pose suffocation risks to children and should be stored high up in a locked cupboard where children cannot reach them. The sharp edges of aluminum foil, plastic wrap, and waxed paper boxes can also injure children and should be stored away from reach. If your child ever grabs something sharp, do not try to pull it out of her hand. Squeeze her wrist firmly until she lets go of the sharp object.

There is a huge array of electrical appliances in the kitchen that are hazardous to children. Kitchen stoves, refrigerators, ovens, microwaves, and dishwashers can all lead to burns and other injuries. Blenders, toasters, and coffee makers are also possible causes of injury to children. They should be secured with guards, latches, and straps to prevent access, and guard against injury. Unplug electrical appliances when not in use, and store appliances pushed toward the back of the counter with electrical cords out of reach.

Every year thousands of children are injured due to tipping furniture and appliances. Stoves and refrigerators are among the items that children have pulled down onto themselves. Heavy and/or unstable furniture should be removed or secured with special furniture straps to studs in the walls to prevent them from tipping onto a child. Refrigerator doors should be latched closed to prevent being pulled onto a child. Be sure to install tip-resistant feet onto your stove/oven if the manufacturer supplied them, or contact the manufacturer for recommendations on securing the stove/oven to minimize tipping.

Cabinet & Drawer Latches:

Installing latches on cabinets and drawers can be one of the most time consuming tasks a parent endures. Cabinet and drawer latches are especially important in rooms like the kitchen and bathroom where medicines, cleaners, cosmetics, and other potentially poisonous substances are stored. These harmful items should be moved to a cabinet or drawer that is out of reach of children and is securely locked. Install latches on each cabinet and drawer that holds harmful items including sharp objects, poisonous objects, breakables, and other items children should not have access to. The tools needed to install cabinet and drawer latches are a drill and a screwdriver. Before beginning the installation of cabinet &

drawer latches, make sure you put on eye protection and have a screwdriver and drill with several sizes of drill bits ready for use.

There are several types of cabinet & drawer latches that include a template for easier installation:

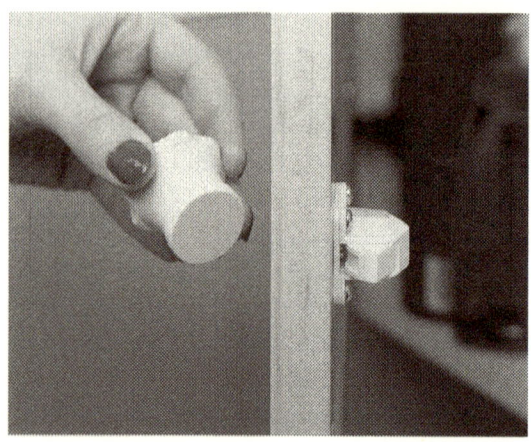

Tot-Lok Magnetic Lock by Rev-A-Shelf

and

Adhesive Mount Cabinet Lock by Kidco, Inc. requires no screws

A good bet cabinet & drawer latch for most types of cabinets and drawers a type that states that they will work for framed and frameless (European style) cabinets.

With a little bit of preparation, and some time and patience, the kitchen can be made into a "Totsafe" area for your child.

- Install a baby safety gate to prevent access to the kitchen, especially when cooking.

- Determine which cabinet & drawer types you have (framed or frameless) and install latches on all cabinets & drawers.

- Move all cleaners, plastic bags, etc. to locked, high cupboards.

- Protect children from burns from stoves using a Stove Guard and remove stove knobs or install stove knob locks or covers.

- Use the back burners when cooking and NEVER hold your child while cooking.

- To keep children from accessing unsafe items in the fridge, install a lock to prevent access. Children also my try to climb the shelves inside the fridge—a lock will help prevent climbing, too.

- Be sure anti-tip devices are installed on your oven/stove and refrigerator.

- Never allow your child to have access to sharp objects such as knives, scissors, plastic wrap boxes, etc.

- Place all appliances out of reach or attach them to the counter using safety appliance straps.

7

Bathroom Safety

Bathrooms hold a whole host of child safety issues that need to be dealt with. Here is a list of the most common problem areas in the bathroom:

Toilets: Children are particularly curious about water, even water in the toilet. Just a couple of inches of water, such as that in the toilet, bucket, or pet dish can pose a drowning risk. Use toilet locks to prevent access to water in the toilet, and never keep water in buckets, tubs, etc. Most toilet locks will work on any style of toilet, but should specify in the description if certain styles will not work. Most toilet locks do not require the use of any drills or screwdrivers, and should be easily opened and closed. Some require the use of adhesive, some, like the Lid-Lok (shown below) clamp to the bowl of the toilet for superior strength.

Lid-Lok Toilet Lock by Mommy's Helper, Inc.

Water sources (faucet, bathtub, shower): Children should not have access to water for many reasons. In addition to the drowning risk associated with water, it can also put children at risk for being scalded if it is too hot. Water heaters in your home should be set to no more than 120 degrees to help prevent this. Keep bathroom doors closed or gated off and use a Safety Tap Guard to prevent access to water.

Cabinets/Drawers: Cabinets and drawers hold many items that can be dangerous to children including cleansers, medicines, cosmetics and sharp objects like knives and scissors. Cabinets and drawers should be secured with locks or latches to prevent access. Individuals who prefer not to install hardware mounted cabinet & drawer latches can try Adhesive Mount Cabinet Latches. See Chapter 4 for information on choosing and installing cabinet locks.

Garbage Cans: Children should not have access to garbage cans or their contents. Garbage cans should be placed where children cannot reach them, and locked closed with a locking strap.

Medicines, Cleaners, Cosmetics, etc.: These items should to be kept out of the reach of children. Medicines, cosmetics, cleaners and other household products should be kept in their original containers with labels, and up in cupboards or on shelves where children cannot have access to them. Use cabinet locks and latches on cupboards or drawers where these items are stored.

Nightlights: Some nightlights have small parts and hot bulbs that can injure children. They also may be pulled out, exposing children to outlets.

- Nightlight with Outlet Cover is an alternative to standard nightlights, and offers protection from outlets.

Use childproofing products correctly all of the time. Train older children, babysitters and visitors (including Grandma & Grandpa) on how to properly use child safety items in your home to help ensure correct use, and continued protection of your child. It only takes one time for a cabinet to be left open, or a toilet to be left unlocked for an accident to happen.

Prevent access to scalding water using anti-scald devices, and/or setting your water heater to a maximum temperature of 120 degrees and always supervise your child in the bath. Installing a slip-resistant bathtub mat will also help prevent slips and falls in the bathtub for you and your child.

- Install toilet locks on all toilets in the home and teach everyone how to use them correctly and consistently.

- To keep children out of the bathroom, simply install a lock on the door out of the reach of children.

- Turn your hot water heater to a maximum of 120°F to prevent scalding.

- Never allow your child to have access to water in the sink, tub, toilet, or buckets.

- Install cabinet & drawer latches on all cupboards and drawers.

- Place garbage cans inside locked cupboards.

- Place all medicines, cleaners, cosmetics, etc. out of reach in high, locked cupboards.

- Place electrical safety products on all electrical outlets.

8

Furniture & Fireplaces

Tip-Resistant Furniture Safety Brackets by Mommy's Helper, Inc.

Furniture in the home can be hazardous to young children. Sharp edges and corners, unstable furniture, and heavy items on top of furniture can all create unsafe environments for curious infants, toddlers, and young children. It is estimated that 8,000-10,000 children are injured every year in furniture tip-over accidents.

There are many steps that can be taken to help prevent accidents from sharp edges and corners of furniture and fireplaces. It is important to remove any glass-top tables, end tables, etc. as children have fallen into these types of tables and been severely injured. Sharp corners and edges can be padded with special table and hearth edge cushions. These cushions can be cut to fit any size and shape, and most are installed using double sided adhesive tape. Do not use corner cushions alone—small children will pull them off easily and expose the sharp corners.

Install anti-tip furniture straps or brackets into studs in the wall to all dressers, armoires, bookcases/bureaus, entertainment centers, etc. to help prevent tipping. These straps are generally easy to install using a screwdriver, drill, and a stud finder. Mount one side into the piece of furniture and one side into a stud in the wall. Connect the two sides with the special strap to help prevent the piece of furniture from tipping.

Remove heavy equipment (like TVs, stereos, etc.) from tabletops to prevent equipment from toppling onto children. Heavy equipment can also be strapped to tabletops and entertainment centers with Anti-Slip Safety Straps. Remove toys, trinkets, etc. from tabletops to prevent children from trying to climb to reach these items.

There are many types of fireplace hearth padding and safety items. I highly recommend installing a fireplace safety gate that will completely block off access to the fireplace and keep children away from the dangerous fireplace hearth.

HearthGate™ by Kidco, Inc.

The HearthGate™ by Kidco, Inc. can be secured at both ends into the walls around the fireplace, has a door for parent-access to the fireplace, and helps keep kids away from the fireplace, hearth, and fireplace accessories like pokers, matches, and wood. The gate will fit hearths up to six feet wide and two feet deep, and extensions can be added easily to fit larger areas. The HearthGate™ is also a good option for gating off barbecue areas.

If you want to provide protection without the bulk of a hearth gate, you may want to take a look at hearth padding to soften the edges and corners of the hearth and also install a lock on the fireplace doors to keep little ones from opening the fireplace when you're not around. Most fireplace door locks cannot be kept on when you're using the fireplace, so never use the fireplace when your little one is around unless you've got a hearth gate.

There are so many brands and types of fireplace hearth padding that it'd be impossible to discuss them all in this book. Fireplace hearth padding comes in many different shapes, sizes, and colors. Here are some tips to help you choose fireplace hearth padding:

- **Measure your fireplace hearth**—this is the most important thing you need to know when you go out to purchase hearth padding

- **Determine what type of material your hearth is made of**—it could be traditional brick, stone, marble, or almost any other material imaginable.

- **If your hearth has a chalky texture to it, a hearth pad that uses adhesive to stay on probably will not work**—you'll need to find a product like the Kid's Edge Metal Backed Hearth Guard by Cardinal Gates that actually clamps to the hearth rather than using adhesive tape.

- **When working with adhesive tape, be sure to thoroughly clean the area before attempting to make it stick**—and try to install it before your child is old enough to notice it. If you install it when your little one is 20 months old, it's likely that he or she will be curious and try to pull it off.

- **Purchase extra adhesive tape**—just in case your little angel decides to see what's under the padding. Some manufacturers sell additional tape and most hardware stores carry tape that will work just fine. One of my friends has had good luck with carpet installation tape.

Kid's Edge Metal Backed Hearth Guard by Cardinal Gates

- Install anti-tip furniture straps on all furniture including dressers, armoires, entertainment centers, bookcases, etc. to prevent tipping.

- Attach electronic devices such as TVs, microwaves, etc. to stable furniture using anti-slip safety straps.

- Remove small and breakable items from tabletops and shelves.

- Install a fireplace safety gate around fireplaces or install fireplace hearth padding and a fireplace door lock to prevent injuries.

- Use corner & edge cushions on all sharp edged tables, window ledges, etc.

9

Nursery Safety

From electrical outlets to heavy furniture, to bi-folding closet doors and rubber tipped door stops, creating a safe nursery environment for your child can be overwhelming and leave you screaming for a family bed. But don't give up your comfortable sleeping just yet. Creating a safe room for your child can be easy if you know what to look for.

One of the most important things that you can do in your child's room is to position the crib in a space where your child will not be able to reach anything from inside. Keep the crib away from windows and out of reach of window blinds, blind cords, curtains, electrical outlets, and anything else that he or she could reach for. Remember, for young children there should be no objects in the crib other than your baby. Never use a crib that is missing parts or that has slats further than 2 3/8 inches apart from each other.

Be sure to install outlet covers, plates or plugs in all electrical outlets in the room. If you have a baby monitor or other appliance plugged in most of the time, I recommend using an outlet safety cover (see Chapter 4 for more information). Use outlet plugs in outlets that are rarely used and using Sliding Outlet Plates in almost any area. Do not plug any type of appliance into an outlet located close to the baby's crib.

When little ones get older, they may have unattended wandering time in their bedrooms, so it is especially important to install anti-tip furniture brackets to dressers, bookshelves, etc. to prevent tipping. Children often pull out dresser drawer drawers and use them as steps to get to whatever is on top of the dresser. Remove all objects of interest from tops of furniture to help prevent climbing, and install cabinet/drawer latches on drawers and cabinets found in the bedroom.

Window safety is an important topic when talking about nurseries. Thousands of children are injured every year due to falls from windows; even first story window falls can be fatal to children. Install Window Guards on all windows that children will have access to, and never leave windows open when a child is unattended. Window Guards are quite easy to install with the use of a drill and screwdriver. Simply measure your window opening and purchase a guard made to fit that measurement. Windows that can be opened more than 4" pose a hazard to children. Window Wedges that help prevent windows from being opened past a certain point can also be installed, with minimal effort and cost.

It is important to either cut or move window blind cords so that they are out of the reach of children. Window blind cords are a strangulation hazard to children, and if possible should be removed from the home. Any ointments, etc. that are stored in a child's room should be removed as soon as your little one learns to stand up, as climbing out of the crib may soon follow, and these products can be poisonous if ingested. Be sure to remove the diaper pail if plastic bags are used in it at the same time.

Some nightlights have small parts and hot bulbs that can injure children. They also may be pulled out, exposing children to outlets. The Nightlight with Outlet Cover is an alternative to standard nightlights, and offers protection from outlets in addition.

Be sure that a working smoke detector and carbon monoxide detector are placed near all sleeping areas of the home in case of fire or carbon monoxide exposure. Installing smoke detectors can easily be done with a drill and screwdriver, and most carbon monoxide detectors can be plugged into an outlet (just make sure your child can't access it and pull it out).

Check behind your child's bedroom door, and you're likely to find one of the largest choking hazard culprits that I know of—the doorstop. If your doorstop has a rubber tip on the end, remove the rubber tip immediately. It is easily pulled off by you, and easily pulled off by a child, who may put it in his mouth. One-piece rubber doorstops can be installed in place of this type of doorstop and have no pieces that can be removed.

If your child's bedroom has a changing table in it, be sure to attach the changing table to the wall to help prevent tipping if your child attempts to crawl up it. Remove all medicines, cleaners, ointments, and plastic bags (including diaper pail bags) from the room.

Is there a bathroom connected to your child's bedroom? Use a child safety lock on the bathroom door to keep children from being able to have access to the bathroom unattended. Use a toilet lock on the toilet even if there is a lock on the bathroom door, and make sure all cleaners and cosmetics are removed from reach and secured in a locked cabinet.

Once you've created a safe bedroom environment for your child, one of the most difficult issues for parents is how to keep their little one in their bedroom.

One of the best ways to prevent unattended wandering throughout the home when your child should be in his/her bedroom is to install a child safety gate in the doorway of his or her bedroom. Use a safety gate that your child cannot remove or crawl over, and check to make sure it is properly and securely installed before each use. If your child is likely to push toys over to the gate and attempt to crawl over it, install two gates, one on top of the other to make a very tall "door-type" gate. Make sure you use a baby safety monitor to hear what is happening in your child's bedroom at all times, and if possible, use a video monitor so that you can also see what is going on. Some baby monitors are "two-way" monitors that allow you to hear your child, and allow you to speak to your child by pushing a button on the handset. This can be a very useful feature of a monitor and can help your little one feel more secure in his/her bedroom environment.

- Place crib in a safe place, away from windows, furniture, etc. Don't hang anything from the wall or ceiling around the crib.

- Windows and window blinds are a hazard to children—secure windows with locking guards and remove window blinds with cords, or at least place the window blind cords out of reach.

- Make sure your child's crib is up to the most recent safety standards—never purchase a used crib or use a crib with missing parts.

- Install electrical outlet safety products in all outlets.

- Place door locks on bi-fold doors to prevent pinches.

- Install anti-tip furniture safety straps to all dressers, armoires, etc. to prevent tipping.

- Place all electrical cords out of reach.

- Install latches on cabinets & drawers.

- Remove all ointments, creams, diaper pails, etc. before your child is able to climb out of her crib.

- Install a working smoke detector and carbon monoxide detector in all sleeping areas of the home.

- Remove all small objects, including door stops with rubber tips.

- Place a lock on any bathrooms attached to your child's room so she can't access the bathroom unattended.

- Install a safety gate in the doorway to help prevent unattended wandering once your child is in a "big-kid" bed or can climb out of the crib.

- Discontinue use of the crib before you child can climb out of it.

- Use a monitor at all times when your child is in her room to help you hear you child in her room.

10

Emergency Medical Treatment

It's one of a parent's worst nightmares—you're sitting at the dinner table and all of the sudden you notice that your child is choking. Thankfully you took a child CPR class (right?! If you haven't yet, you should) and are able to remove the blockage safely before any harm is done.

Would you know what to do if your precious little one started exhibiting signs of choking? Or seizures? Or what if your toddler had an accident and started to bleed? How to respond in the even of an emergency is one of the most important things a parent can learn. Most hospitals and many other agencies have free or low cost classes for parents to learn emergency response techniques such as CPR (cardiopulmonary resuscitation) and many offer CPR classes specifically for parents of infants and young children. To locate classes in your area, log on to the American Hearth Association website at http://www.americanheart.org. I also recommend purchasing a "cheat sheet" of emergency responses like CPR for infants and placing it in an easily accessible area like the refrigerator. Check with your pediatrician for this type of information. Some may give them to parents for free, and most can help you locate one. At the end of this book, you will find a list of other important telephone numbers and forms for you to fill out to prepare you in the event of an emergency.

As a parent of a young child, you need to be aware of the most common injuries to children and familiarize yourself with how to identify and treat these injuries. According to the American Heart Association, choking, burns, drowning, and Sudden Infant Death Syndrome (SIDS) are some of the most common injuries occurring to young children in the home. Falls are also a main cause of injury to children. One of the most important things you can do in order to successfully treat a child with an emergency medical condition is to remain calm. It may seem impossible to stay calm when your child's life is at risk, but it is absolutely necessary. You will not be able to properly care for your child if you become extremely distressed. Also, remember to call your emergency support number (generally 9-

1-1) immediately and explain the situation as thoroughly, but quickly, as possible.

CHOKING:

Food is a common cause of choking among children. In addition to food, there are several other items around the home that are commonly overlooked:

- Rubber tips from doorstoppers.

- The small cap at the base of the toilet.

- Coins—Check under those couch cushions often!

- Balloons.

- Older siblings' toys—keep those Barbie shoes out of reach.

- Loose cabinet and drawer pulls.

- Chewing gum.

- Marbles.

- Food. Never leave children unattended while eating.

- Leaves and stones in household plants.

- Pen and marker caps—Keep your purse out of reach!

- Small batteries.

- Medicine bottle caps.

- Some older outlet plugs.

- Plastic wrapping, like bubble wrap and plastic food wrap. DVD & CD wrappers can cause problems, too.

- Peanuts—just the right size to block a child's airway.

- Grapes & hotdogs are huge culprits in child choking accidents and should be cut into small pieces to prevent choking.

BURNS:

Installing smoke detectors and checking (and replacing) the batteries in those smoke detectors is one of the best and most efficient ways to help prevent burns to children. According to the American Heart Association, 70% of deaths of fire and burn-related deaths occur in homes without working smoke detectors.

Injuries due to burns can come from many sources commonly found in the home. Some of the most common sources of burns (and scalding) to children are items that are used on a daily basis and should be kept away from children or blocked from children's access:

- **Stoves & ovens**—use locks and guards to help prevent access. Never hold your child while you are cooking, and always use the back burners. Keep pot and pan handles out of children's reach.

- **Bathtub, shower & sink water** (set your hot water heater to 120 degrees Fahrenheit or less to help prevent scalding).

- **Candles**—Keep candles out of the reach of children.

- **Cigarettes**—children can be severely burned by touching cigarettes.

- **Matches & Lighters**—even small children can light matches or lighters. Keep them out of the reach of children and use "child resistant" lighters.

- **Curling Irons**—keep curling irons and cords out of the reach of children—never use one while holding your child.

- **Hot liquids & foods**—coffee, tea, soups, etc. are all burn/scald hazards to children. Never hold your child while preparing or handling these items. Keep children away when handling these items.

- **Hot water vaporizers**—use a cold water vaporizer instead.

- **Electrical appliances & cords**—properly secure all electrical outlets and cords out of children's reach. Do not allow your child to chew on an electrical cord.

- **Fireplaces**—install guards to keep children away from fireplaces or only use the fireplace after your child has gone to bed.

This is just a small list of some of the common burn hazards in the home. There are hundreds (if not thousands) of items in the home that can burn a child. Look around your home and remove as many of these things as possible. If you haven't done it lately, please check the batteries in your smoke detectors and replace them at least every six months.

DROWNING:

Children are fascinated with water—have you ever noticed how a child will inevitably find a puddle to splash in even in his/her best Sunday outfit? Unfortunately, drowning is one of the most common causes of death in children under the age of four, and most drowning deaths could have been prevented. With a few precautions, the risk of drowning can be dramatically decreased. The most common areas in the home with water are:

• **Swimming Pools**

• **Toilets**

• **Bath Tubs**

• **Water Buckets**

• **Sinks**

• **Animal Dishes**

It is very important to secure these areas away from children. Swimming pools should be fenced with locking mechanisms on the gate so that children cannot access them without proper adult supervision. Never leave your child in or around water for any length of time for any reason. Children can drown in a matter of moments. Designate an appropriate person to watch your child if you cannot and keep all ride-on toys away from the pool area.

Water in the toilet is an especially hazardous area for children. Young children may "play" with the water in the toilet, and may put their heads into the toilet bowl, but most do not have the strength to get themselves out and may drown. It is essential to keep children away from water in the toilet by keeping bathroom doors closed and locked and installing locking mechanisms on all toilets in the home. Instruct all individuals in the home (including visitors and babysitters) on the proper use of safety items to ensure their proper use even when you are not home.

Children can drown in just a few inches of water. Water in tubs, buckets, sinks, and animal dishes must be kept away from children. Children should NEVER be left alone in the bathtub—not even for a few seconds. Children's bathtubs, slings, etc. should not be used as safety devises, and do not use any product that uses suction cups to attach to the bottom of your tub. They may come loose and tip your child into the water.

SUDDEN INFANT DEATH SYNDROME (SIDS):

According to the American Sudden Infant Death Syndrome Institute, Sudden Infant Death Syndrome is the sudden, unexplained death of an infant under the age of one year. Most of these deaths occur while the child is sleeping, which leads many researchers to believe that SIDS is caused by a lack of air.

Although SIDS is not completely understood, there are some things that have been found to help decrease the risk of SIDS:

- Place your infant to sleep on his/her back.

- Use a firm mattress, and never allow any soft items such as blankets, pillows, stuffed animals or crib bumpers in the crib. Dress your baby in an appropriate sleeper.

- Do not expose your baby to tobacco smoke.

- Dress your baby in just enough clothing to keep warm—do not overdress your baby.

- If your baby is at high risk for SIDS, ask your doctor about appropriate monitoring devices to help detect breathing problems during sleep.

FALLS:

I have heard people say, "Children fall down all the time, and it's just a part of growing up." Fortunately, most falls are not serious, and often result in bumps and bruises that are not of large concern. The type of falls that are of major concern to child safety are generally not from the regular bumps and bruises of learning to walk. Falls down stairs, out of cribs, in shopping carts, and even off of the couch can have a profoundly negative impact on a child's health and well-being and should be prevented as much as possible. Young children are especially vulnerable to falls and should be supervised to help prevent injuries.

It is important to know that if your child falls and begins to act abnormally, such as vomiting, won't stop crying, abnormal breathing,

strange color, etc. call your child's doctor or an emergency number (often 9-1-1) immediately.

Some of the most common areas/products related to falls are:

- **Stairways**—properly secure stairways so children do not have access to them unattended. Keep stairways free of toys, etc. and never allow a young child to carry toys, blankets, etc. up or down the stairs, as they may trip and fall because of them.

- **Cribs**—older children may attempt to climb out of or into the crib—move your child to a toddler bed or safer bed as soon as your child exhibits signs of climbing or if the edge of the crib is at or below your child's shoulder level.

- **Highchairs, swings, etc.**—always securely strap your child into a highchair or swing to help prevent falls. Never allow your child to climb into or out of a highchair or swing.

- **Shopping Carts**—never place an infant car safety seat on the top of a shopping cart. Properly secure children who are old enough to sit unattended in the seat of a shopping cart and do not allow older children to stand on the side or end of the cart or push the shopping cart.

- **Falls from couches, tables, etc.**—Never leave your newborn or young child unattended on couches, tables or beds—even newborns can kick or wriggle and may fall from areas such as couches and tabletops. Never put your child in a car seat, bouncy seat, etc without properly securing with the straps.

- **Table or Fireplace Hearth edges and corners**: Falls onto sharp table or fireplace edges and corners can be particularly hazardous to children and often result in emergency room visits. Install edge and corner cushions to pad the edges to soften and absorb shock.

11

Family Safety—ideas to keep your whole family safe at home

Child safety is an important topic for parents—but sometimes parents overlook important ways to keep the entire family, including themselves, safe. There are many ways in which parents can make the home safer for everyone.

Have a fully stocked all-purpose first aid kit in the home to help ensure that you have what you need in the event of an emergency. There are some first aid kits that have been developed with the guidance of the American Medical Association to make certain that the essentials are included.

A fully stocked first aid kit should include a cold compress, antiseptic cleansing pads, assorted sizes of adhesive bandages, roll bandages, sponge pads, sterile eye pads, sting relief pads, tweezers, scissors, tape, latex gloves, antibiotic ointment, burn relief gel, and a first aid booklet to help you know what to do in the event of an injury. It's also important that you talk to your pediatrician to find out what medications you should have on hand to keep your baby or young child safe in the event of an emergency.

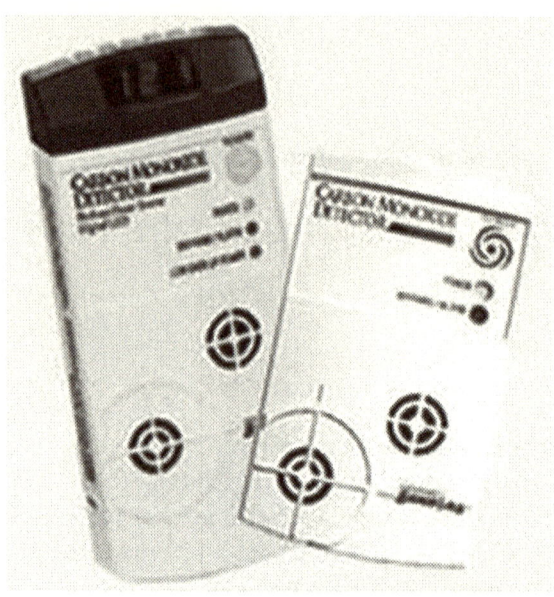

Carbon Monoxide Detectors by Dicon Global, Inc.

Carbon monoxide is a colorless, odorless gas that is of particular hazard to children because they have faster metabolic rates than adults and gas accumulates faster in their bodies than adults. It is recommended that carbon monoxide detectors be placed on each floor of the home. I recommend placing one in every separate sleeping area as well. Don't forget to install smoke detectors on every floor in the home and around each sleeping area—and check the batteries often.

Does your home have more than one story? Do you have an escape plan if a fire breaks out in your home? Does the entire family know what to do in the event of a fire? Create a fire escape plan today and share it with older children in the home. Be sure to include instructions regarding how to get out of the house if there is a fire, testing doors for heat before opening them, how to put out a fire if your clothes catch fire, etc. Have fire drills for older children to ensure that they understand the plan. Make sure that you talk to your children about the importance of not playing with matches, etc. and to never hide from a fire!

Most home fires start in the kitchen. It is important to remember to never leave food cooking in the kitchen unattended and that you keep your stove and oven's cooking surfaces clean to help prevent fires. Keep combustible materials such as potholders, washcloths, paper towels, etc. away from hot stove surfaces as they can easily catch fire. Also, make sure to clean out your dryer's lint trap after every load. Make sure to remove the lint trap at least weekly and clean it with a scrub brush under warm water to remove any film that's accumulated there. Experts also recommend vacuuming the insides of the dryer slot to remove any material that has gotten past the lint trap.

Fire Escape Safety Ladder by Kidde

A fire escape ladder or other way out of the house is a necessity to ensure safe escape from a burning home. There should be a fire escape ladder in every bedroom in the home and every person in the home should know how to use the ladder. Another important fire safety tip is to install child locator decals on bedroom windows where children sleep to help fire fighters locate areas where children may be sleeping. These stickers are not approved for use in some areas, check with your local fire department or police department to see if the stickers are allowed.

Do you know what's in the water you're drinking? There can be hundreds (if not thousands) of bacteria and unwanted poisons in your home's drinking water. Water testing can be ordered for free or a low cost at local health departments to determine the water quality. Test for radon, pesticides, lead, and for levels of fluoride, etc. Ask your doctor and health department for advice to help determine appropriate levels and to evaluate the water quality.

If there was an emergency at your home and you called for the police, fire department or an ambulance, you would expect that they should be able to find your home. But if your house numbers are not clearly visible from the road, the emergency service may drive right past your house and may not be able to find you. I highly suggest using house numbers on your home that are in contrast to the color of your house. It is also a good idea to place your house numbers on your mailbox or at the end of your driveway. If you live in an apartment, make sure that your apartment number is easy to find at the entrance doorway.

12

Home Childproofing Checklist

The following is a list of common child safety risks in the home. Check off items once they are removed or secured.

☐   **Stairways**: Secure the top and bottom of stairways with baby safety gates to prevent falls and unattended access. Please see the "GUIDE TO BABY SAFETY GATES CHAPTER" to help you choose which gates are right for your space and to help you determine where to put baby safety gates. <u>PRESSURE MOUNTED BABY GATES ARE NOT RECOMMENDED FOR THE TOP OF THE STAIRS.</u> Special Circumstances (molding/baseboards, uneven or hollow walls, wrought iron railings, balusters, etc.) may require the use of gate installation kits to create a mountable surface.

☐   **Windows**: All windows, even first floor windows, pose a falling hazard to children. Windows should not be able to be opened more than 4". Children should not have access to open windows. Use childproofing window guards on second story and higher windows, use window safety devises to prevent the window from opening more than 4".

☐   **Window Blinds**: Cords from window blinds are a strangulation risk to children and can easily be removed or secured out of reach. NEVER PLACE A CHILD'S CRIB OR BED NEAR THE WINDOW OR WINDOW BLINDS. I highly suggest removing window blinds from your home that have cords—especially in rooms where your child may be left unattended. If removal is not an option, cut the cord (there should be NO loops) and secure any extra cord out of reach. Even the inner cord of window blinds can be a strangulation risk, so be sure to never leave a child unattended, especially in a room with window blinds.

☐   **Outlets**—Create a barrier between children and electrical currents with appropriate childproofing measures. Often, furniture can be strategically placed to hide electrical outlets.

Determine whether your outlets are Standard (one screw) or Decorator (two screws) and:

- If you have outlets constantly in use (i.e. lamp plugged in all the time): Install an outlet cover.

- For outlets that are frequently used (i.e. outlet used to plug in vacuum, then remove it): Try sliding outlet plates, which replace your existing outlet plate and have a 'door' that slides closed to cover the outlet as soon as an item is unplugged.

- For outlets that are rarely used (normally left unused): Outlet plugs fit snugly inside outlets to prevent access.

Medicines, Cleaners, Cosmetics, etc.: These items are poisonous and should to be kept out of the reach of children in a locked cabinet. Medicines, cosmetics, cleaners and other household products should be kept in their original containers with labels, and up in cupboards or on shelves where children cannot have access to them. Use cabinet locks and latches on cupboards or drawers where these items are stored. If your child ever ingests poisonous materials call a Poison Control Center or emergency services immediately. Have the substance in hand when you call.

Open Banisters: Remove items from around banisters, half walls, etc. that children may use to climb. This includes toys, chairs, tables, and other products that curious children may use to step up on. Use clear, plastic banister shields to close off gaps between balusters and newel posts, particularly where the space is more than 4".

Kitchens: Kitchens can be one of the most hazardous rooms in your home. If it is possible, use a baby safety gate to block off access to the kitchen, especially during cooking or baking.

- Always use the back burners when cooking; make sure that panhandles are pointing toward the back of the stove.

- Never hold your child while in the kitchen. Children may try to grab hot foods or sharp items that could injure them. If a child does grab a sharp item such as a knife, <u>do not</u> try to pull it out of the child's hand. Instead, firmly squeeze the child's wrist until they let go of the object.

- Use Stove Knob Covers or Locks to prevent access to burner knobs—without them children may turn on the gas of the stove or turn on the stove creating burn and fire hazards.

- Use adhesive locks on the refrigerator/freezer to prevent little ones from getting into food & drinks (and plastic and glass containers) they should not have.

- Keep knives and other sharp objects stored in locked drawers.

- Store plastic bags away from children.

Electrical Appliances: There is a huge array of electrical appliances that are hazardous to children. Kitchen stoves, refrigerators, ovens, microwaves, and dishwashers can all lead to burns and other injuries. They should be secured with guards, latches, and straps to prevent access, and guard against injury. Heavy appliances (stove & fridge) should be secured to the wall to prevent tipping.

Heavy or Unstable Furniture (including dressers, armoires, stoves, refrigerators, entertainment centers, book cases and changing tables, etc.): Every year thousands of children are injured due to tipping furniture and appliances. Children pull out dresser drawers and use them as steps to climb up furniture. Heavy and/or unstable furniture should be removed or secured with special furniture straps to studs in the walls to prevent them from tipping onto a child. Keep the tops of furniture clear of knick-knacks, toys, flowers, etc. to help deter climbing.

Water Sources: Children are particularly curious about water, even water in the toilet. Just a couple of inches of water, such as that in the toilet, bucket, or pet dish can pose a drowning risk. Use toilet locks to prevent access to water in the toilet, and never keep water in buckets, tubs, etc. Pets' water dishes should be kept out of the reach of babies and toddlers as well. In addition to the drowning risk associated with water, it can also put children at risk for being scalded if it is too hot. Water heaters in your home should be set to no more than 120 degrees to help prevent this. Keep bathroom doors closed or gated off and use a safety tap guard to prevent access to water.

Cabinets/Drawers: Cabinets and drawers hold many items that can be dangerous to children including cleansers, medicines, cosmetics and sharp objects like knives and scissors. Cabinets and drawers should be secured with locks or latches to prevent access. Individuals who prefer not to install hardware mounted cabinet & drawer latches can try latches that are mounted with adhesive or latches that clamp over cabinet knobs requiring no screws or adhesive.

Garbage Cans: Children should not have access to garbage cans or their contents. Garbage cans should be placed where children cannot reach them, and locked closed with a locking strap.

Sharp-edged tables or fireplace hearths: Use corner and table edge cushions to pad sharp edges of tables, hearths, computer desks, counters, etc. to help prevent bumps, bruises, and other injuries.

Cords in reach: cords should be kept out of reach of children to minimize pulling on items, gaining access to electrical outlets, and minimize strangulation risks associated with cords. Computers, entertainment centers, telephones, and lamps are a few of the items that have cords that should be secured out of reach. Cord control kits or outlet covers with cord shorteners can be used for this purpose.

Nightlights: Some nightlights have small parts and hot bulbs that can injure children. They also may be pulled out, exposing children to outlet receptacles.

- Nightlight with Outlet Cover is an alternative to standard nightlights, and offers protection from outlets.

Fireplaces, Wood Burning Stoves, Barbecue Grills: Children should not be allowed near fireplaces, grills or wood burning stoves. It is good practice not to allow children near them even when they are not in use. Protect children from burns from fireplaces and stoves with fireplace gates. Use edge and corner cushions on hearths to protect from bumps and bruises.

Plants: Several household plants can be fatal to children if eaten, and the fertilizer in soil can be harmful, as well. Plants should be moved out of children's reach. If that is not an option, pots should be covered with mesh or plastic so that child does not have access to the soil. Your local hardware store should be able to help you find an appropriate gauge of mesh so that children can't reach in, but allow plants to 'breathe.' Plants can also fall off tables or be knocked over if heavy.

TV/VCR/DVD/Stereo: Children are often fascinated with buttons and doors, such as those found on TVs, VCRs, etc. Clear plastic shields can be used to guard against having a child insert inappropriate items into the VCR, push buttons, etc. Attach appliance straps to items to help prevent them from tipping onto children.

☐ **Computer and Entertainment Centers**: Areas around the computer and entertainment centers can have several hazards to children. Generally, these areas have a large amount of cords, adapters, and heavy equipment like a monitor or television set. Browse our website for power strip safety covers, outlet & adapter covers, cord control kits, and safety locking straps to help prevent injuries.

☐ **Carbon Monoxide & Smoke Detectors**: It is recommended by the Consumer Products Safety Commission that carbon monoxide detectors be placed in every separate sleeping area of the home. Carbon monoxide is a colorless, odorless gas, which is a particular hazard to children because they have faster metabolic rates and gas accumulates faster in their bodies than adults. There should be at least one smoke detector on every floor of the home, with properly installed and working batteries.

☐ **Swimming Pools**: Swimming pools are a main source of danger for children, who are naturally curious about water. Pools (and other sources of water) should be secured with pool fences. If a door leads to the swimming pool area, it should be locked with a door lock that the child is unable to defeat.

Other Home Child Safety Tips:

☐ Use childproofing products correctly all of the time. Train older children, babysitters and visitors (including Grandma & Grandpa) on how to properly use child safety items in your home to help ensure correct use, and continued protection of your child. It only takes one time for a cabinet to be left open, or a toilet to be left unlocked for an accident to happen.

☐ Prevent access to scalding water by using anti-scald devices, and/or setting your water heater to a maximum temperature of 120 degrees.

☐ Make sure cleaners, cosmetics, plants and other poisonous substances are correctly labeled with name and ingredients so that if your baby ingests the item you can give accurate information to a poison control center or emergency medical team.

☐ Always supervise your child in the bath; never leave children alone or with anyone other than a responsible adult.

☐ Remove two-piece doorstops, which have small parts that can be choking hazards, replace with one-piece doorstops.

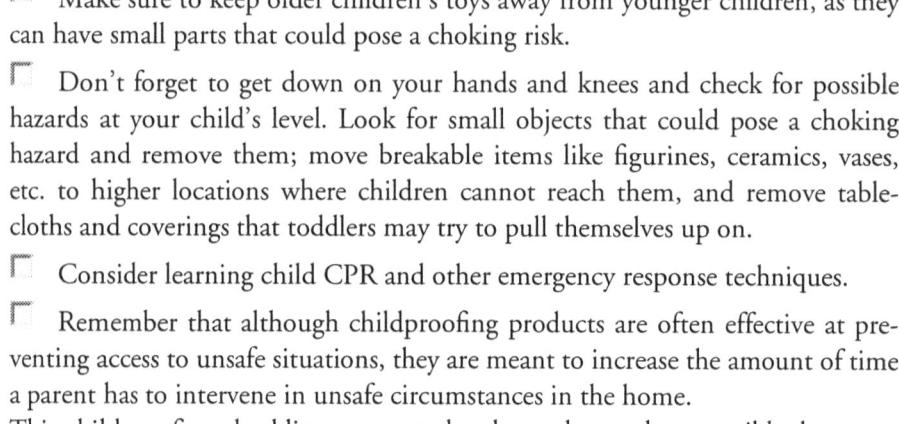

☐   Make sure to keep older children's toys away from younger children, as they can have small parts that could pose a choking risk.

☐   Don't forget to get down on your hands and knees and check for possible hazards at your child's level. Look for small objects that could pose a choking hazard and remove them; move breakable items like figurines, ceramics, vases, etc. to higher locations where children cannot reach them, and remove table-cloths and coverings that toddlers may try to pull themselves up on.

☐   Consider learning child CPR and other emergency response techniques.

☐   Remember that although childproofing products are often effective at preventing access to unsafe situations, they are meant to increase the amount of time a parent has to intervene in unsafe circumstances in the home.

This childproofing checklist was created to be as thorough as possible, however, please remember that this checklist is just for reference, and may not cover all of the child safety issues in your home.

<u>Child safety & childproofing products are meant to be deterrents; they are not meant to substitute for proper adult supervision.</u>

Where do I start?

Where to start can be a frustrating decision for parents. I recommend printing out the above checklist and using it to walk through your entire home. If you can't look at your own home with unbiased eyes, have a friend or neighbor do the walk-through for you. Don't forget to get down on your hands and knees to see what could be lurking under couch edges, tables, etc.

Choosing the right tools for the job will help make any childproofing task easier. Most childproofing can be completed with a drill, screwdriver and several sizes of drill bits. Be sure to wear safety goggles and proper shoes (don't want that drill bit hitting your bare foot!). No experience with a drill? Remove it from it's case, drawer, etc. and practice! Drill practice holes through extra scrap wood. Follow it up by installing screws into the holes that you drilled. You can even practice installing cabinet latches onto a practice scrap of wood to help you get the feel of using the drill and screwdriver.

Start with whatever seems the least daunting, or with what is of greatest concern. If you have a staircase that your newly crawling son likes to practice on even when you're not looking, you may want to focus your efforts there first. Electrical safety items are often the easiest childproofing products to install and don't take long to install.

Conclusion

Parents these days are more educated about child safety than any other generation past. We remember the falls down stairs and the electric shocks. We want to prevent that type of pain from being inflicted on our kids. We were lucky. We made it through the bumps, falls, bruises, and close calls. We don't want our kids to have close calls. Not all children are that lucky—we don't want our kids to be the unlucky ones.

I hope that this book will help you in feeling confident that you can create a safe home environment for your child all by yourself. I suggest printing out the checklist at the end of Chapter 1 and walking around your home with it to figure out what needs to be done. You will find many more resources, and all of the products that are mentioned in this book on my website, at http://www. totsafe.com. I'm also available to answer specific questions via email. Just log onto the website and click the "Contact" button. If you have questions about products or how to install them, please ask. I'll be happy to help you on your way to creating a "Totsafe" home.

All product pictures in this book are courtesy of the manufacturers. Special thanks to:

- *Cardinal Gates, Inc.*

- *Kidco, Inc.*

- *Summer Infant*

- *Safety 1st*

- *Mommy's Helper, Inc.*

- *Prince Lionheart*

- *Parent Units*

- *Rev-A-Shelf*

- *Kidde*

- *Dicon Global, Inc.*

Frequently Asked Childproofing Questions

"I need a child safety gate for the top of a staircase but one side is wall and the other is a metal handrail (wrought iron). I cannot use a pressure system because of the stair use and I cannot use a hardware mount system because of the metal railing side. What can I do?"

A wrought iron railing is common in stairways of many older homes and apartments. For mounting a gate to this type of railing, try using the Safety Gate Installation Kit K10 by Kidco, Inc., which can be used to create a 'frame' around the wrought iron railing. Hardware mounted gates can then be mounted into this 'frame.'

◆   ◆   ◆

"We have wood sliding closet doors in our daughters room. How can we prevent her from opening them?"

Bedroom closets, and other doors can be secured with door locks to keep them from opening, and to help prevent pinched fingers. For sliding closet doors, try the Sliding Door and Window Lock or Sliding Door Latch. If your closet doors are bi-folding doors, try the Bi-Fold Door Lock.
Have doors with long handles instead of knobs? Secure them with door covers made for lever-style door handles.

◆   ◆   ◆

"What's the recommended maximum distance between banisters?"

As a general rule, banisters that have vertical or horizontal openings wider than 4" can pose a safety risk for children. This includes banisters inside and outside of the house. Banister guards—clear plastic shields, can be attached to banisters to close off the gaps and help prevent accidents from falls through the railings and from becoming stuck in the railings. Banister guards also help prevent children from climbing up balusters.

◆   ◆   ◆

"Should we use something on the stairs to help keep our 3 year old from slipping?"

Absolutely. Using a non-slip stairway runner can help your little one climb up and down the stairs without slipping. Stairway runners can be purchased at most hardware stores. Please be sure to continue to supervise your little climber closely when she's climbing the stairs, even with a non-slip runner. This is still only practice and she should not be allowed to climb without supervision for quite some time.

◆   ◆   ◆

"How can we baby proof our kitchen without installing all of those cabinet & drawer latches?"

Whenever possible, we recommend blocking off the kitchen with a baby safety gate, especially while you are cooking. Installing and consistently using a baby safety gate in the doorway or entryway of your kitchen would eliminate the need for cabinet & drawer latches (and refrigerator & oven latches, stove knob covers, etc). Be sure to read the manufacturers instructions to ensure proper installation and use of the gate, and discontinue use of the gate when the gate is at or below your child's shoulder level.

◆   ◆   ◆

"How is your lazy susan latch installed? Is it screwed in or is it an adhesive?"

The Lazy Susan Latch by Safety 1st is screwed in with two screws on the side of the cabinet frame. The latch "clamps" around the lazy susan door, keeping it from opening in both directions. The lazy susan doors must be a part of the lazy susan, not the type that first open, and the lazy susan is behind. This latch does not work on cabinet frames with beveled edges.

◆   ◆   ◆

"I need to buy several of the sliding safety plate outlet covers, but I want to be sure I'm getting the right ones."

There are three different types of sliding safety plates for outlets: One type for standard outlets with two prongs, one for standard outlets with three prongs, and one for decorator outlets (two screw) with three prongs. Each item is designated as to which type of outlet it is for, and the product pictures illustrate it further.

Did you know that there is a difference between standard and decorator outlets? Standard outlets have one screw in the middle. Decorator, or Decora®, outlets have two screws, one at the top and one at the bottom. Most outlet safety products are designed for standard outlet styles.

◆   ◆   ◆

"We have a gas fireplace and the light switch for it is rather low. Our 2 1/2 year old can easily reach it. Is there any sort of light switch protector that you know of?"

The Switch-Lock Guard by Safety 1st helps prevent children from being able to operate both standard and decorator switches of lights, fireplaces, garbage disposals, etc.

◆   ◆   ◆

"I am looking for something to go around my treadmill. Any suggestions?"

The Kidco Configure Gate G80 generally works well for childproofing the space around a treadmill and other exercise equipment. Unlike standard baby safety gates that only mount in a straight line, the Kidco Configure Gate G80 can be customized to fit almost any shape and size that you need. It's good for around treadmills, to surround stairways, blocking off entryways, even around Christmas trees.

◆   ◆   ◆

We have a dresser where our twin toddlers' clothes are kept. The dresser has three drawers (each one above the other) that slide out; however, there is no space (or piece of cabinetry) between the drawers. Any ideas would be greatly appreciated.

Many types of cabinet latches include a 'catch' that can be used for most styles of cabinets and drawers, including frameless styles like those in dressers. Also included is a template to make installation a breeze! You may want to install the latches on the side of the dresser drawers to make operating the latches easier. Another important issue to mention when discussing dressers is installation of tip-resistant furniture safety brackets to help prevent the tipping of furniture, such as dressers, onto children. Furniture safety brackets or straps help attach the piece of furniture to a stud in the wall with a strong, nylon or plastic strap to prevent tipping.

◆   ◆   ◆

"I'm worried that my daughter will get burned on the wall heater in her bedroom and on other ones throughout the house. What can I do to help keep her away from it?"

Wall heaters are a common concern for parents. Many models can become hot to the touch, and they may have sharp edges that children can become hurt on. We often recommend that parents try to 'barricade' wall heaters from children by placing furniture in front of the heater—if you decide to do this, be sure to keep the furniture away from the heater enough so that it doesn't pose a fire hazard. A second option is to block off the heater with a baby safety gate like the Configure Gate® by Kidco, Inc. Be sure to mount the gate far enough from the heater that baby cannot reach in and touch the heater.

◆   ◆   ◆

"We have been looking for a safety gate we can use at the top of our stairs on our outside deck. We have been unsuccessful and were hoping you could give us a name of a gate that is safe to use on our deck."

There are several gates available for use in outdoor stairway locations, depending on the size that you need:

For a stairway opening 27" to 42 ½" (add extension to fit spaces up to 64") check out the Cardinal Gates Stairway Special. The Kidco Safeway Gate will fit spaces 24 ¾" to 43 ½" and you can add extensions to fit spaces up to 66". The Kidco Configure Gate is also available for use outdoors, includes 3 24" panels, and you can add extension panels to fit any size and shape opening that you need.

All of these gates are approved for use outdoors. They must be treated with a rust-inhibiting product (like Rustoleum®) to prevent rust, and should be removed in extremely cold weather.

Important Resources for Parents regarding Child Safety & other child related topics

National Capital Poison Center

Mailing Address:
3201 New Mexico Ave.
Suite #310
Washington, DC 20016
http://www.poison.org
EMERGENCY: 1-800-222-1222

American Academy of Pediatrics

Mailing Address:
141 Northwest Point Boulevard
Elk Grove Village, IL 60007-1098
USA
Tel: 847-434-4000
Fax: 847-434-8000
http://www.aap.org

American Heart Association

Mailing Address:
7272 Greenville Avenue
Dallas, TX 75231
Tel: 1-800-AHA-USA-1 (1-800-242-8721)
http://www.americanheart.org

Consumer Products Safety Commission

Mailing Address:
U.S. Consumer Product Safety Commission
4330 East West Highway
Bethesda, MD 20814
Tel: 800-638-2772
Fax: 301-504-0124 and 301-504-0025
E-mail: info@cpsc.gov
http://www.cpsc.gov

Juvenile Products Manufacturers Association

Mailing Address:
15000 Commerce Pkwy.
Suite C
Mt. Laurel, NJ 08054
Tel: 856-638-0420
Fax: 856-439-0525
E-mail: jpma@ahint.com
http://www.jpma.org

Safe Kids Worldwide

Mailing Address:
1301 Pennsylvania Ave., NW
Suite 1000
Washington, DC 20004-1707
Tel: 202-662-0600
Fax: 202-393-2072
http://www.safekids.org

National Highway Traffic Safety Administration

Mailing Address:
400 Seventh Street, SW
Washington, DC 20590
Toll-Free: 1-888-327-4236
TTY: 1-800-424-9153
http://www.nhtsa.gov
http://www.seatcheck.org

American Sudden Infant Death Syndrome Institute

Mailing Address:
509 Augusta Drive
Marietta, GA 30067
Tel: 770-426-8746
Toll-Free: 800-232-SIDS
Fax: 770-426-1369
http://www.sids.org

National Safety Council

1121 Spring Lake Dr.
Itasca, IL 60143-3201
(800) 621-7619
(630) 285-1121
(630) 285-1315 fax
http://www.nsc.org
Customer Service: **customerservice@nsc.org**

About the Author

Where I grew up in rural Michigan there was no formal childproofing. No one installed outlet plugs into outlets or baby safety gates at the tops of stairs. No one removed the sharp edged tables or tipsy furniture. I have vivid memories of being shocked by an electrical outlet at my grandmother's house and falling down the stairs (probably in the same day)—luckily no broken bones were suffered, although I do remember not being able to breath for several moments. Childhood was fun, innocent, and sometimes painful. We hit our heads on table corners receiving injuries that probably should have been stitched, but alas, that was what being a kid was all about, right?

Growing up in farm country made me learn something that most women don't learn—we can do things that require the use of power tools and construction ability. I worked with my father for several summers of my childhood on a dairy farm feeding and milking cattle, bailing hay, and moving the cows from barn to pasture. The moment you walk behind a herd of stubborn cattle and motivate them to go out to the pasture, something clicks and you realize that you can do pretty much anything. You feel like you could build a bridge or create a new design for a luxury car. Luckily, childproofing does not require extensive knowledge of building codes nor does it require a degree in engineering. You can create a "Totsafe" home with little or no prior experience, although if you have experience with tools or construction, "You go, girl!"

I've been in the business of keeping kids safe for over six years now, but it's been a passion for many years more than six. In the beginning, I was working for a high-end baby specialty store. The store sold safety items, but unfortunately, there weren't a lot of qualified people in the store to sell the products, including myself, and most of the selling was focused on toys, layette items, and strollers. There was some, but very little, training to teach us to help new parents select child safety items. We weren't taught that specific child safety gates fit specific situations, and that some kids will learn how to pull electrical outlet plugs out of the outlet within minutes of Mom and Dad installing them for the first time. Most of the sales staff did not have children, and like myself, had never seen these products in action. Needless to say, there was a large amount of returns on child safety items in that store.

About one year after I began working for the store, I became the Store Manager and decided that my entire staff, myself included, should begin focusing on increasing our knowledge of the child safety items in the store—we knew that child safety was the number one concern of our clientele, but we didn't know how to help them keep their children safe. I started little by little reading product packaging and learning about the different products and their uses. I researched different products through the Internet and found countless websites devoted to child safety and injury prevention, but I remember being overwhelmed by the amount of information. I couldn't imagine how parents sort through all the information to find the right products and information to keep kids safe.

Within a few months, I became pregnant with my son (who at the time of this writing is now 4). As like most parents, child safety immediately became the number one priority for me, and it was no longer a work project, it was (and is) my life. I was immediately concerned with what I needed to do to help keep my little one safe while he was growing in his protected environment and it wasn't long before I started thinking about keeping him safe after he finally arrived.

My attention pointed to the topics of child safety and childproofing. I read constantly about infant and toddler safety and spoke with other parents and co-workers throughout the company about their experiences. I discussed the topic with doctors, nurses, and countless other professionals, and none were able to give me specific answers to childproofing questions. Although everyone wants kids to be safe, it seems that none of these professionals actually knew how to do it.

Shortly after my son was born, I returned to my work as a Store Manager and returned to helping other parents keep their children safe—but with a renewed interest in the child safety aspect of the business. I worked with a local hospital to start holding childbirth education classes with a registered nurse in the store, and on one evening of each session, we discussed child safety products. We focused on how to select proper car seats, and when and what to childproof at home when baby got older. It was exciting to help these new parents learn what would help them keep their future babies safe.

Helping new parents learn how to keep their children safe is now my number one priority. I stopped working for the child specialty store and I now own a childproofing company and child safety website, called Totsafe, (we're online at http://www.totsafe.com) that is dedicated to providing high quality childproofing and toddler safety products to parents, grandparents, and caregivers. The website's mission is to provide childproofing products that fit any home, style, and budget. We strive to help increase awareness of toddler safety issues in the home, in hopes of decreasing risk of injury during this stage of amazing milestones and endless curiosity.

I also install the childproofing products that I sell and, most importantly, I train parents and caregivers on their appropriate use. I am committed to providing parents with child safety products and resources in order to help keep children safe at home and hope that this book will help you on your journey of child safety.

978-0-595-41076-7
0-595-41076-6

www.ingramcontent.com/pod-product-compliance
Lightning Source LLC
Chambersburg PA
CBHW020345290526
45785CB00005B/2167